MODERNITYSCOTLAND

HIGHER POLITICS

COURSE BOOK

John McTaggart

TABLE OF CONTENTS

4	**INTRODUCTION**
5	**POLITICAL THEORY**
29	**POLITICAL SYSTEMS**
51	**POLITICAL PARTIES AND ELECTIONS**
74	**THE COMPARISON QUESTION**
84	**THE VIEWPOINT QUESTION**

INTRODUCTION

Welcome to the Higher Politics coursebook!

This book enables you to develop your skills in answering the questions in the SQA Higher Politics papers. The companion is quite simple.

For each question highlight the key words in the question.

Refer to the relevant section in the

www.higherpolitics.scot

Learning Management System

Write down the key points to mention in the Planning Box.

Attempt the answer using the prompts provided.

Succeeding in Higher Politics is about learning the course content, knowing where the marks come from and practicing each type of question till you feel confident.

POLITICAL THEORY:

12 MARK QUESTION

Analyse the key features of direct democracy. (12)

Write three well explained paragraphs which are detailed and accurate, with an example in each one.

Make comments about the relationship between direct and indirect democracy too, this shows analysis, which you need in order to gain full marks.

Go to: **www.higherpolitics.scot**

PLANNING BOX

ANSWER

A key feature of direct democracy is making decisions. In a direct democracy...

_____

_____

_____

_____

_____

_____

For example...

_____

_____

_____

_____

_____

_____

_____

_____

ANSWER

Whereas, in a representative democracy such as the UK House of Commons...

_____
_____
_____
_____
_____
_____
_____
_____
_____
_____
_____

For example...

_____
_____
_____
_____
_____
_____
_____
_____
_____
_____

ANSWER

Another key feature of direct democracy is that it tends to be used in referenda.

_____

_____

_____

_____

_____

_____

_____

_____

_____

_____

_____

For example...

_____

_____

_____

_____

_____

_____

_____

_____

_____

_____

ANSWER

In a representative democracy, referenda may not be the best way to make a law. This is because...

_____

_____

_____

_____

_____

_____

_____

_____

_____

_____

_____

For example...

_____

_____

_____

_____

_____

_____

_____

_____

_____

_____

ANSWER

A last key feature of direct democracy is the power given to voters...

_____

_____

_____

_____

_____

_____

_____

_____

_____

_____

_____

For example...

_____

_____

_____

_____

_____

_____

_____

_____

_____

_____

ANSWER

Whereas, in a representative democracy, elected representatives have more power because...

_____
_____
_____
_____
_____
_____
_____
_____
_____
_____
_____

For example...

_____
_____
_____
_____
_____
_____
_____
_____
_____
_____
_____

CONCLUSION. DO NOT SIMPLY RESTATE YOUR POINTS, BUT MAKE COMMENTS ON SIMILARITIES/DIFFERENCES IN THE POINTS YOU HAVE MADE.

Joseph Schumpeter in his book 'Capitalism, Socialism and Democracy' was very negative about both direct and indirect democracy. He believed....

_____

_____

_____

_____

_____

_____

_____

_____

For example...

_____

_____

_____

_____

_____

_____

_____

_____

12 MARK CHECKLIST

Have I written three paragraphs about key features? ☐

Are these paragraphs detailed and accurate? ☐

Does each paragraph contain an example? ☐

Have I mentioned key theorists and their publications? ☐

Have I made analytical comments? ☐

POLITICAL THEORY:

20 MARK QUESTION

To what extent are there similarities between the key features of political ideologies? (20)

The 20 mark question is a much trickier question than the 12 marker.

First, you need a plan of what you are going to write as your essay must have a structure and a line of argument. State this line of argument in your introductory paragraph.
(2 marks).

You must have an overall conclusion where you return to your line of argument and support it, with fresh content. Do not just 'sum up', write something new which supports your line of argument
(4 marks).

Lastly, in the main body of your essay, have three paragraphs which explain the differences and similarities between the different ideologies and make evaluative comments about them. (14 marks, 8 for knowledge and understanding and 6 for analysis).

Go to www.higherpolitics.scot

PLANNING BOX

Answer: Introduction / Line of Argument

In this essay I shall discuss the extent to which there are similarities between the ideologies of conservatism and socialism. My line of argument shall be...

_____

_____

_____

_____

_____

_____

_____

_____

_____

_____

_____

_____

_____

Answer: Knowledge & Understanding

One major difference is in attitudes towards society. The socialist Jimmy Reid, in his famous address to Glasgow University students argued that...

_____

_____

_____

_____

_____

_____

_____

_____

_____

_____

Answer: Knowledge & Understanding

This can be compared with Conservative Prime Minister Margaret Thatcher. In her famous speech 1987 speech where she argues that...

_____

_____

_____

_____

_____

_____

_____

_____

_____

_____

_____

_____

_____

_____

_____

_____

_____

_____

_____

_____

Answer: Analysis / Line of Argument

The differences are vast. Reid supports...

_____

_____

_____

_____

_____

_____

Whereas Margaret Thatcher believed the exact opposite...

_____

_____

_____

_____

_____

This supports my line of argument that...

_____

_____

_____

_____

_____

Answer: Knowledge & Understanding

Another major difference is in the ideologies' approach to social change. Edward Burke, the classic conservative theorist believed...

_____

_____

_____

_____

_____

_____

_____

_____

_____

_____

_____

_____

_____

_____

_____

_____

_____

_____

_____

_____

Answer: Knowledge & Understanding

This approach to change can be contrasted with that of Vladimir Lenin, the Marxist leader of the Russian revolution. He believed that...

_____

_____

_____

_____

_____

_____

_____

_____

_____

_____

_____

_____

_____

_____

_____

_____

_____

_____

_____

Answer: Analysis / Line of Argument

The differences are enormous. Marxists believe...

_____

_____

_____

_____

_____

Whereas conservatives such as Burke and Oakeshott believe the exact opposite...

_____

_____

_____

_____

_____

This supports my line of argument that...

_____

_____

_____

_____

_____

Answer: Knowledge & Understanding

The last major difference is in the ideologies' approach to the role of government. Fabian socialists believe...

_____

_____

_____

_____

_____

_____

_____

_____

_____

_____

_____

_____

_____

_____

_____

_____

_____

_____

_____

_____

Answer: Knowledge & Understanding

This approach to government can be contrasted with that of Margaret Thatcher's Conservative governments. They succeeded in...

_____

_____

_____

_____

_____

_____

_____

_____

_____

_____

_____

_____

_____

_____

_____

_____

_____

_____

_____

Answer: Analysis /Line of Argument

The differences are vast. Fabian and Labour socialists believe...

_____

_____

_____

_____

_____

Whereas Thatcherite conservatives believe the exact opposite...

_____

_____

_____

_____

_____

This supports my line of argument that...

_____

_____

_____

_____

_____

Answer: Conclusion: Analysis / Line of Argument

Not all socialists and conservatives believe in the opposite. Fabian socialists and 'one nation conservatives' can find common ground as they both believe...

_____

_____

_____

_____

_____

_____

_____

_____

_____

_____

_____

_____

_____

_____

_____

_____

_____

_____

_____

_____

_____

Answer: Conclusion: Analysis /Line of Argument

However, my line of argument is that, in general, socialists tend to look at society from a different viewpoint from conservatives...

20 MARK CHECKLIST

Does my Introduction explain my line of argument?

Are my paragraphs detailed and accurate?

Does each paragraph contain an example?

Have I made analytical comments about the differences/similarities?

Have I mentioned key theorists and their publications?

Does my conclusion support my line of argument with new content (not repeating what I've already written)?

POLITICAL SYSTEMS:

12 MARK QUESTION

Compare the role of the legislature in passing legislation in two political systems you have studied. (12)

Write three well explained paragraphs which are detailed and accurate, with an example in each one.

Make a comment about the degree of difference too, this shows analysis, which you need to gain full marks.

Go to www.higherpolitics.scot

PLANNING BOX

ANSWER

There are many differences in the passage of legislation between the UK Parliament and the US Congress.
One difference is in the role of the Executive. In the UK...

_____

_____

_____

_____

_____

_____

_____

_____

_____

_____

_____

For example...

_____

_____

_____

_____

_____

_____

_____

_____

_____

_____

ANSWER

Whereas, in the US Congress, the Executive has a very different role...

_____

_____

_____

_____

_____

_____

_____

_____

_____

_____

_____

For example...

_____

_____

_____

_____

_____

_____

_____

_____

_____

_____

ANSWER

Another difference is in the role of the party whips. In the UK...

_____

_____

_____

_____

_____

_____

_____

_____

_____

_____

For example...

_____

_____

_____

_____

_____

_____

_____

_____

_____

ANSWER

Whereas, in the US Congress, the party whips, traditionally, have had a very different role...

_____
_____
_____
_____
_____
_____
_____
_____
_____
_____
_____
_____

For example...

_____
_____
_____
_____
_____
_____
_____
_____
_____
_____

ANSWER

A third difference is in the role of the second chamber. In the UK, the House of Lords...

_____

_____

_____

_____

_____

_____

_____

_____

_____

_____

_____

For example...

_____

_____

_____

_____

_____

_____

_____

_____

_____

ANSWER

Whereas, in the US Congress...

_____

_____

_____

_____

_____

_____

_____

_____

_____

_____

_____

For example...

_____

_____

_____

_____

_____

_____

_____

_____

_____

_____

12 MARK CHECKLIST

Have I written three paragraphs which show difference? ☐

Are these paragraphs detailed and accurate? ☐

Does each paragraph contain an example? ☐

Have I made analytical comments? ☐

POLITICAL SYSTEMS:

20 MARK QUESTION

To what extent are there differences between the key features and importance of constitutions? (20)

The 20 mark question is a much trickier question than the 12 marker.

First, you need a plan of what you are going to write as your essay must have a structure and a line of argument. State this line of argument in your introductory paragraph.
(2 marks).

You must have an overall conclusion where you return to your line of argument and support it, with fresh content. Do not just 'sum up', write something new which supports your line of argument
(4 marks).

Lastly, in the main body of your essay, have three paragraphs which explain the differences and similarities between the different constitutions and make evaluative comments about them. (14 marks, 8 for knowledge and understanding and 6 for analysis).

Go to www.higherpolitics.scot

PLANNING BOX

Answer: Introduction/Line of Argument

In this essay I shall discuss the extent to which there are differences between the UK and US constitutions. My line of argument shall be...

_____
_____
_____
_____
_____
_____
_____
_____
_____
_____
_____
_____
_____
_____
_____
_____
_____
_____
_____
_____
_____
_____
_____
_____
_____
_____
_____

Answer: Knowledge and Understanding

One major difference is whether a constitution is codified or uncodified. The UK's Constitution is uncodified. This means...

_____

_____

_____

_____

_____

_____

_____

_____

_____

_____

_____

_____

_____

_____

_____

_____

_____

_____

_____

_____

_____

_____

_____

_____

_____

Answer: Knowledge and Understanding

This can be compared with the American constitution which is written and contained in one document.

_____

_____

_____

_____

_____

_____

_____

_____

_____

_____

_____

_____

_____

_____

_____

_____

_____

_____

_____

_____

_____

_____

_____

_____

Answer: Analysis /Line of Argument

This difference is very important because...

_____
_____
_____
_____
_____
_____
_____
_____
_____
_____
_____

This supports my line of argument that...

_____
_____
_____
_____
_____
_____
_____
_____
_____
_____
_____
_____
_____
_____

Answer: Knowledge and Understanding

Another major difference is how the two constitutions came into existence. Democracy in the UK is very different to democracy in the USA in terms of how it was created.The Constitution, therefore, is very different....

_____

_____

_____

_____

_____

_____

_____

_____

_____

_____

_____

_____

_____

_____

_____

_____

_____

_____

_____

_____

_____

_____

_____

Answer: Knowledge & Understanding

Whereas, democracy in the USA was created in a very different manner and the country's Constitution plays a very different role...

Answer: Analysis /Line of Argument

This difference is very important because...

_____

_____

_____

_____

_____

_____

_____

_____

_____

This supports my line of argument that...

_____

_____

_____

_____

_____

_____

_____

_____

_____

_____

_____

_____

Answer: Knowledge & Understanding

A last major difference is how the Constitutions protect individual rights. Individual rights are absolutely central to American politics and Government.....

_____

_____

_____

_____

_____

_____

_____

_____

_____

_____

_____

_____

_____

_____

_____

_____

_____

_____

_____

_____

_____

_____

_____

_____

_____

_____

_____

Answer: Knowledge & Understanding

This can be compared with the UK, where individual rights are not so well protected...

Answer: Analysis /Line of Argument

This difference is very important because...

_____
_____
_____
_____
_____
_____
_____
_____
_____
_____

This supports my line of argument that...

_____
_____
_____
_____
_____
_____
_____
_____
_____
_____
_____
_____
_____
_____
_____

Answer: Conclusion: Analysis /Line of Argument

Throughout this essay, my line of argument has been.....

_____

_____

_____

_____

_____

_____

_____

_____

_____

When you compare the UK and US constitutions you can see how this is is clear

_____

_____

_____

_____

_____

_____

_____

_____

_____

_____

_____

_____

20 MARK CHECKLIST

Does my Introduction explain my line of argument? □

Are my paragraphs detailed and accurate? □

Does each paragraph contain an example? □

Have I made analytical comments about the differences/similarities? □

Does my conclusion support my line of argument with new comments (not repeating what I've already written)? □

POLITICAL PARTIES AND ELECTIONS:

12 MARK QUESTION

Analyse the effectiveness of campaign management techniques. (12)

Write three well explained paragraphs which are detailed and accurate, with an example in each one.

Make comments about the effectiveness of campaign management techniques. too, this shows analysis, which you need in order to gain full marks.

Go to www.higherpolitics.scot

PLANNING BOX

ANSWER

A campaign management technique is the use of the leader's popularity. In the 2015 UK General Election, the SNP consistently promoted Nicola Sturgeon...

_____

_____

_____

_____

_____

_____

_____

_____

_____

_____

_____

For example...

_____

_____

_____

_____

_____

_____

_____

_____

_____

_____

_____

ANSWER

This was effective because....

_____
_____
_____
_____
_____
_____
_____
_____
_____
_____
_____
_____
_____
_____
_____
_____
_____
_____
_____
_____
_____
_____
_____
_____
_____
_____
_____

ANSWER

A different campaign management technique is the use of technology such as Nationbuilder. In the 2015 UK General Election, the SNP used this software. What Nationbuilder does is...

_____

_____

_____

_____

_____

_____

_____

_____

_____

_____

For example...

_____

_____

_____

_____

_____

_____

_____

_____

_____

_____

_____

_____

ANSWER

This was effective because....

_____

_____

_____

_____

_____

_____

_____

_____

_____

_____

_____

_____

_____

_____

_____

_____

_____

_____

_____

_____

_____

_____

_____

_____

ANSWER

A final campaign management technique is the use of technology such as Activate. In the 2015 UK General Election, the SNP used this software. What Activate does is...

_____

_____

_____

_____

_____

_____

_____

_____

_____

For example...

_____

_____

_____

_____

_____

_____

_____

_____

_____

_____

ANSWER

This was effective because....

_____

_____

_____

_____

_____

_____

_____

_____

_____

_____

_____

_____

_____

_____

_____

_____

_____

_____

_____

_____

_____

_____

CONCLUSION. DO NOT SIMPLY RESTATE YOUR POINTS, BUT MAKE COMMENTS ON THE OVERALL EFFECTIVENESS.

In the 2015 General Election, the SNP ran a very professional campaign which used a range of different methods, each of which played their part in delivering the party's best result ever......

12 MARK CHECKLIST

Have I written three paragraphs about campaign management techniques?

☐

Are these paragraphs detailed and accurate?

☐

Does each paragraph contain an example?

☐

Have I commented on why they were effective?

☐

POLITICAL PARTIES & ELECTIONS
20 MARK QUESTION

To what extent is the sociological model more relevant in explaining voting behaviour than other models in the UK? (20)

The 20 mark question is a much trickier question than the 12 marker.

First, you need a plan of what you are going to write as your essay must have a structure and a line of argument. State this line of argument in your introductory paragraph.
(2 marks).

You must have an overall conclusion where you return to your line of argument and support it, with fresh content. Do not just 'sum up', write something new which supports your line of argument
(4 marks).

Lastly, in the main body of your essay, have three paragraphs which explain whether you believe the sociological model is more relevant than other models of voting behaviour. (14 marks, 8 for knowledge and understanding and 6 for analysis).

Go to www.higherpolitics.scot

PLANNING BOX

Answer: Introduction/Line of Argument

In this essay I shall discuss whether the sociological model more relevant in explaining voting behaviour than other models in the UK My line of argument shall be...

Answer: Knowledge & Understanding

The sociological model is relevant in analysing modern voting behaviour because social class is still a big factor in UK elections...

_____

_____

_____

_____

_____

_____

_____

_____

_____

_____

_____

_____

_____

_____

_____

_____

_____

_____

_____

_____

_____

Answer: Knowledge & Understanding

However, the sociological model cannot explain everything. Supporters of the Party Identification Model would point out that...

_____

_____

_____

_____

_____

_____

_____

_____

_____

_____

_____

_____

_____

_____

_____

_____

_____

_____

_____

_____

_____

_____

Answer: Analysis /Line of Argument

However, this does not mean that the sociological model is out dated....

_____

_____

_____

_____

_____

_____

_____

_____

_____

_____

This supports my line of argument that...

_____

_____

_____

_____

_____

_____

_____

_____

_____

_____

_____

_____

_____

Answer: Knowledge & Understanding

One other reason why the sociological model remains of value today is the impact of age on voting behaviour...

_____

_____

_____

_____

_____

_____

_____

_____

_____

_____

_____

_____

_____

_____

_____

_____

_____

_____

_____

_____

Answer: Knowledge & Understanding

Age, however, cannot explain everything. Critics of the sociological model would point out...

_____

_____

_____

_____

_____

_____

_____

_____

_____

_____

_____

_____

_____

_____

_____

_____

_____

_____

_____

_____

_____

_____

_____

Answer: Analysis /Line of Argument

The sociological model is not perfect. There are valid criticisms of it to be made. However....

_____

_____

_____

_____

_____

_____

_____

_____

_____

_____

This supports my line of argument that...

_____

_____

_____

_____

_____

_____

_____

_____

_____

_____

_____

_____

Answer: Knowledge & Understanding

One more reason why the sociological mode remains relevant is due to race...

_____

_____

_____

_____

_____

_____

_____

_____

_____

_____

_____

_____

_____

_____

_____

_____

_____

_____

_____

Answer: Knowledge & Understanding

However, while race is undoubtedly an issue in modern behaviour, how decisive a factor is it?

_____

_____

_____

_____

_____

_____

_____

_____

_____

_____

_____

_____

_____

_____

_____

_____

_____

_____

_____

_____

Answer: Analysis /Line of Argument

We can see that there are many different issues at work in modern elections and voting behaviour is a very complex issue.

_____

_____

_____

_____

_____

_____

_____

_____

_____

_____

_____

This supports my line of argument that

_____

_____

_____

_____

_____

_____

_____

_____

_____

_____

Answer: Conclusion: Analysis /Line of Argument

Throughout this essay, my line of argument has been.....

_____

_____

_____

_____

_____

_____

_____

_____

When you compare the different models of voting behaviour, you can see the continued relevance of the sociological model.

_____

_____

_____

_____

_____

_____

_____

_____

_____

20 MARK CHECKLIST

Does my Introduction explain my line of argument? ☐

Are my paragraphs detailed and accurate? ☐

Does each paragraph contain an example? ☐

Have I made analytical comments about the relevance of the sociological model compared with other models of voting behaviour? ☐

Does my conclusion support my line of argument with new comments (not repeating what I've already written)? ☐

COMPARISON QUESTION

In this type of question you will be presented with two text based sources.

You will then be asked to make three points of comparison between them and come to an overall conclusion.

There is no need for any background knowledge or information, you must use only the text based sources provided.

It is advisable that you take a new paragraph for each point of comparison (and also for your overall conclusion) to make it clear to marker that you have identified three different points.

You'll find a highlighter pen very handy for this question!

For full marks you must reach an overall conclusion.

COMPARISON QUESTION

Study Sources A and B, then answer the question which follows.

Socialists' Views on the UK Monarchy

Socialists believe that the monarchy is an institution which is out of date. As far back as the eighteenth century, countries such as France and the USA rejected the idea of inherited power. Rejecting superstitious ideas of 'divine rights to rule' they chose instead to be representative democracies where power lies with the people, not some King or Queen whose lifestyle is set apart from the rest of society. Similarly, in the 20th century the vast majority of nations which emerged from colonial rule chose to be republics instead of monarchies. No one today would choose to be a subject rather than a citizen. Deference towards our supposed 'betters' is a relic of the past.

Socialists support equality. That means equality of opportunity for all people of all backgrounds to achieve their potential and a greater equality in the share of resources so that we all begin life from a more equal starting point. States which have a monarchy send a message to society that some people are more important, or better than others. The monarch represents class privilege. No wonder that so many people in the UK lack self-esteem or ambition when the state celebrates the fact that some people, through inheritance and not their talents are socially superior to the rest of the population.

COMPARISON QUESTION

Socialists believe the UK royal family is completely undemocratic.

The Queen is the head of state. She makes political interventions such as her comments during the Scottish independence referendum.

Prince Charles has access to the Government that no ordinary member of the public has and we have no way of knowing how much influence he has.

Socialists believe that all those who hold power should be elected and accountable to the voters. It is time that we had an elected head of state, one who can represent the country because he/she is one of the people, not a privileged aristocrat who knows nothing of the lives most of us lead.

Source B: Conservatives' Views on the UK Monarchy

The UK monarchy plays no role in politics. Conservatives believe in democracy. We believe that Parliament, not the monarch, is sovereign. The monarch's role today is ceremonial, indeed its great strength is that it is 'above politics'. No one knows the political views of the royal family. Their job is to represent the nation; all parts and peoples of our nation and they do it very well. Far from being out of touch, the modern royal family has evolved over time. Today's young royals are considerably more popular than our politicians! They do a fantastic job, raising money for a wide range of voluntary causes. They bring a glamour and fun to life which no elected politician could.

Conservatives believe in gradual change. From the French Revolution to Robert Mugabe's Zimbabwe, we have seen the folly and misery of the 'rip it up and start again' approach to constitutional change. We should be careful of what we wish for. The British monarchy is a great source of stability. It is no surprise that throughout the turmoil of the 20th century when all the communist regimes and republics across Europe suffered civil war and occupation, the UK remained united and unconquered. Our royal family has helped keep our nation together. Changing, yes, but not for change's sake. Conservatives support change when it has been properly thought through.

Source B: Conservatives' Views on the UK Monarchy

Conservatives believe that inequality is a fact of life. Some people work harder than others. Some people are more talented than others. The state should not hold people back or penalise those who work hard and earn more. Inequalities in life are nothing to do with the royal family but through some people's inability to make the most of their talents or governmental mismanagement of the economy. Those who criticise the royals should remember how popular the royals are among all sections of society, including those who are disadvantaged. Getting rid of the royal family would make no difference to their lives whatsoever.

Using only the information in Sources A and B. Compare the Socialist and Conservative views on the role of the UK monarchy.

In your answer you must make three points of comparison and reach an overall conclusion. (8)

Answer: Comparison 1

Socialists believe...

_____

_____

_____

_____

_____

_____

_____

_____

_____

Whereas conservatives believe...

_____

_____

_____

_____

_____

_____

_____

_____

_____

Answer: Comparison 2

Socialists believe...

_____

_____

_____

_____

_____

_____

_____

_____

_____

Whereas conservatives believe...

_____

_____

_____

_____

_____

_____

_____

_____

_____

_____

Answer: Comparison 3

Socialists believe...

_____

_____

_____

_____

_____

_____

_____

_____

_____

Whereas conservatives believe...

_____

_____

_____

_____

_____

_____

_____

_____

_____

Answer: Conclusion

My overall conclusion is that...

8 MARK CHECKLIST

Do I have three paragraphs, each with different points of comparison?

Does each paragraph contain an analytical comment on the differences?

Have I taken a final paragraph where I come to an overall conclusion about the Sources?

VIEWPOINT QUESTION

This is a question type which will be based on electoral data. In this type of question you will be presented with up to seven statistical sources.

Then you will read a viewpoint someone has on what the sources represent.

In all likelihood, the viewpoint will have three parts to it, two of which are accurate and one inaccurate, or the other way around.
Your job is to identify the parts of the viewpoint which can be supported by the sources.

Then, come to an overall conclusion on the extent to which the information in the sources support the viewpoint.

There is no need for any background knowledge or information, you must use only the sources provided.

It is advisable that you take a new paragraph for each point (and also for your overall conclusion) to make it clear to marker that you have identified three different points.

You'll find a highlighter pen very handy for this question! For full marks you must reach an overall conclusion.

Study Sources A–G, then answer the question which follows.

Source A: Information on the United Kingdom European Union membership referendum.

The United Kingdom European Union membership referendum took place on 23 June 2016 in the United Kingdom (UK) to ask the people if they wanted the country either to remain a member of or to leave the European Union (EU) under the provisions of the European Union Referendum Act 2015 and also the Political Parties, Elections and Referendums Act 2000.

 The referendum resulted in 51.9% of voters being in favour of leaving the EU. Although legally the referendum was non-binding, the government of that time had promised to implement the result, and it initiated the official EU withdrawal process on 29 March 2017.

The UK was due to leave the EU on 29 March 2019 when the two-year period for Brexit negotiations expired. The so-called Brexit debates have dominated UK politics since 2016 with both Remain and Leave sides claiming public support for their stance.

Source B: Overall Vote in the 2016 EU Referendum

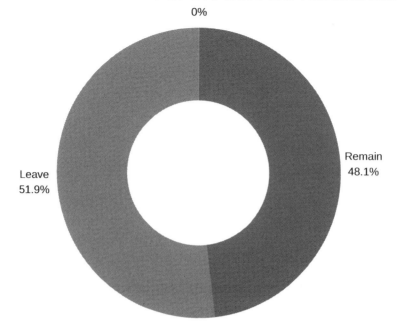

0%

Leave
51.9%

Remain
48.1%

Source C: Voting, across the UK in the 2016 EU Referendum

	Leave	Remain
England	53.4%	46.6%
	15, 188, 406	13,266,996
Scotland	38.%	62%
	1,108,322	1,661,191
Wales	52.5%	47.5%
	854,572	772,347
Northern Ireland	44.2%	55.8%
	349,442	440,707

Source D: Voter turnout in the 2016 EU referendum and recent General Elections

	2015 General Election	2016 Referendum	2017 General Election
UK	66.2%	72.2%	68.7%
England	66%	73%	69.1%
Scotland	71.1%	67.2%	66.4
Wales	65.6%	71.7%	68.8%
Northern Ireland	58.1%	62.7%	65.4%

Source E: Voting, by social class in the 2016 EU Referendum

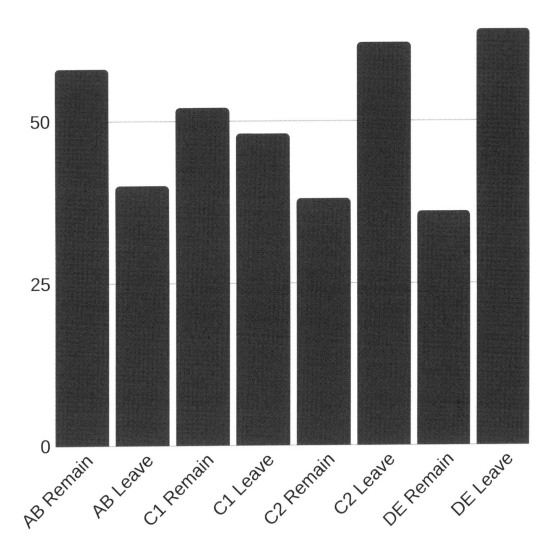

AB = Professional workers C1 = Supervisory workers
C2 = skilled manual workers DE =Unskilled/unemployed

Source F: Voting, by age in the 2016 EU Referendum

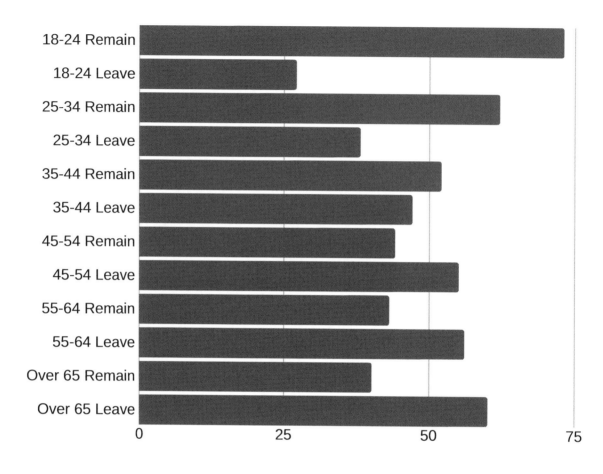

Source G: Opinion poll of UK Voters, March 2019 "In hindsight do you think the UK was right or wrong to vote to leave the EU?"

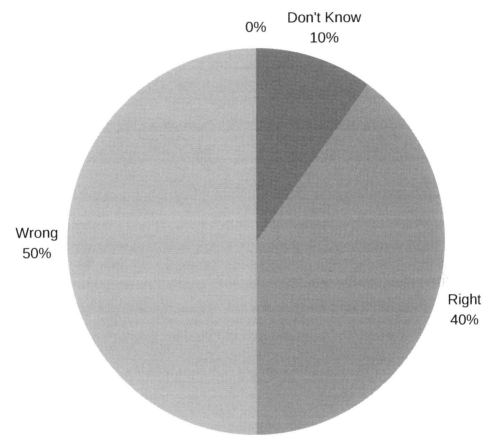

"The 2016 European referendum was a narrow win for the Leave campaign. In all sections of the UK, Leave won the majority of the vote, sometimes by a large majority. Public interest in Brexit was high and there is continued support for the UK to leave."

Using only the information in Sources A-G:

To what extent does the evidence contained in these sources support the viewpoint above? (20)

Answer: Viewpoint

The viewpoint states that the 2016 European referendum was a narrow win for the Leave campaign and it won in all sections of the UK. This is supported by Source B which shows...

_____

_____

_____

_____

_____

_____

_____

_____

_____

This is only partially true. Source C shows...

_____

_____

_____

_____

_____

_____

_____

_____

_____

Answer: Viewpoint

There is a lot of data which does not support the viewpoint. Source E shows that...

_____

_____

_____

_____

_____

_____

_____

_____

However, Source F shows...

_____

_____

_____

_____

_____

_____

_____

_____

_____

_____

Answer: Viewpoint

The viewpoint states that "Public interest in Brexit was high". Source A tells us that the Brexit debates have dominated UK politics since 2016". This is supported by Source D...

_____

_____

_____

_____

_____

_____

_____

_____

_____

However, the viewpoint states that there is "continued support for the UK to leave" which is contradicted by Source G...

_____

_____

_____

_____

_____

_____

_____

_____

_____

Answer: Viewpoint Conclusion

Overall, the viewpoint is mostly valid because...

_____

_____

_____

_____

_____

_____

_____

_____

_____

However, it is not prefect because...

_____

_____

_____

_____

_____

_____

_____

_____

_____

20 MARK CHECKLIST

Have I commented on Source A? ☐

Have I commented on Source B? ☐

Have I commented on Source C? ☐

Have I commented on Source D? ☐

Have I commented on Source E? ☐

Have I commented on Source F? ☐

Have I commented on Source G? ☐

Does my answer address each of the three sentences in the Viewpoint? ☐

Do I have a final paragraph with an overall conclusion on whether the evidence supports the Viewpoint? ☐

Printed in Great Britain
by Amazon

36370785R10054